D1200098

WITHDRAWN FROM
COLLECTION

START
Listening

Sing a Song of Sixpence

Copyright © QEB Publishing, Inc. 2005

Published in the United States by
QEB Publishing, Inc.
23062 La Cadena Drive
Laguna Hills, CA 92653
www.qeb-publishing.com

All rights reserved. No part of this publication may be reproduced, stored
in a retrieval system, or transmitted in any form or by any means, electronic,
mechanical, photocopying, recording, or otherwise, without the prior permission
of the publisher, nor be otherwise circulated in any form of binding or cover other
than that in which it is published and without a similar condition being imposed
on the subsequent purchaser.

Library of Congress Control Number 2005921244

ISBN 1-59566-072-0

Compiled by Anne Faundez
Designed by Melissa Alaverdy
Editor Hannah Ray
Illustrated by Simone Abel

Series Consultant Anne Faundez
Publisher Steve Evans
Creative Director Louise Morley
Editorial Manager Jean Coppendale

Printed and bound in China

START
Listening

Sing a Song
of Sixpence

Compiled by Anne Faundez

QEB Publishing, Inc.

Sing a Song of Sixpence

Sing a song of sixpence,
A pocket full of rye;
Four and twenty blackbirds
Baked in a pie.

When the pie was opened,
The birds began to sing;
Wasn't that a dainty dish
To set before the king?

4

The king was in his counting house,
Counting out his money;
The queen was in the parlor,
Eating bread and honey.

The maid was in the garden,
Hanging out the clothes;
There came a little blackbird
And snapped off her nose.

Little Jack Horner

Little Jack Horner sat in a corner
Eating his Christmas pie,
He put in his thumb and pulled out a plum,
And said what a good boy am I!

Little Miss Muffet

Little Miss Muffet
Sat on a tuffet,
Eating her curds and whey.
Along came a spider
Who sat down beside her,
And frightened Miss Muffet away.

Here We Go 'Round the Mulberry Bush

Here we go 'round the mulberry bush,
The mulberry bush, the mulberry bush,
Here we go 'round the mulberry bush,
On a cold and frosty morning.

This is the way we wash our hands,
Wash our hands, wash our hands,
This is the way we wash our hands,
On a cold and frosty morning.

This is the way we brush our teeth,
Brush our teeth, brush our teeth,
This is the way we brush our teeth,
On a cold and frosty morning.

This is the way we go to school,
Go to school, go to school,
This is the way we go to school,
On a cold and frosty morning.

MORTON MANDAN PUBLIC LIBRARY

One, Two, Three, Four, Five

One, two, three, four, five,
Once I caught a fish alive.
Six, seven, eight, nine, ten,
Then I let it go again.

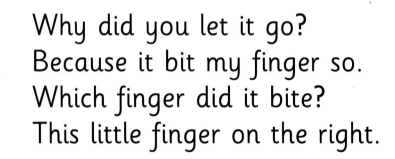

Why did you let it go?
Because it bit my finger so.
Which finger did it bite?
This little finger on the right.

Two Little Dicky Birds

Two little dicky birds
Sitting on a wall;
One named Peter,
One named Paul.

Fly away, Peter!
Fly away, Paul!
Come back, Peter!
Come back, Paul!

Old King Cole

Old King Cole
Was a merry old soul,
And a merry old soul was he.
He called for his pipe and
He called for his bowl,
And he called for his fiddlers three.

Cock a Doodle Doo!

Cock a doodle doo!
My dame has lost her shoe,
My master's lost his fiddling stick,
And doesn't know what to do.

Hush, Little Baby

Hush, little baby, don't say a word,
Mama's going to buy you a mocking-bird.

And if that mocking-bird don't sing,
Mama's going to buy you a diamond ring.

And if that diamond ring turns brass,
Mama's going to buy you a looking glass.

And if that looking glass gets broke,
Mama's going to buy you a billy goat.

And if that billy goat won't pull,
Mama's going to buy you a cart and bull.

And if that cart and bull turn over,
Mama's going to buy you a dog named Rover.

And if that dog named Rover won't bark,
Mama's going to buy you a horse and cart.

And if that horse and cart fall down,
You'll still be the sweetest little baby in town.

Girls and Boys Come Out to Play

Girls and boys come out to play,
The moon doth shine as bright as day,
Leave your supper and leave your sleep,
And join your playfellows in the street;
Come with a hoop, come with a call,
Come and be merry, or not at all,
Up the ladder and over the wall,
A penny loaf will serve us all.

Wee Willie Winkie

Wee Willie Winkie
Runs through the town,
Upstairs and downstairs
In his nightgown,
Rapping at the window,
Crying through the lock,
Are the children in their beds,
For it's now eight o'clock?

17

Hush-a-bye, Baby

Hush-a-bye, baby, on the tree top,
When the wind blows, the cradle will rock;
When the bough breaks, the cradle will fall,
And down will come baby, cradle, and all.

Sleep, Baby, Sleep

Sleep, baby, sleep!
Thy father watches the sheep,
Thy mother is shaking the dreamland tree,
And down falls a little dream on thee.
Sleep, baby, sleep!

How many blackbirds
were baked in a pie?

Can you remember
the names of the two
little dicky birds?

How many things did
Old King Cole call for?

Can you think of
any words that
rhyme with "five?"

Can you name four
things that Mama will
give her little baby?

Can you remember
who lost her shoe?

Can you describe a dream that you would like the dreamland tree to give you?

Who frightened
Miss Muffet away?

Parents' and teachers' notes

- Read through "Sing a Song of Sixpence." Explain to your child the meanings of any of the tricky or unusual words, for example "rye," "dainty," "counting house," and "parlor."
- Ask your child to pretend that he or she is the spider who frightened Miss Muffet away. How would your child approach Miss Muffet? Quietly? Noisily?
- With your child, act out the actions to "Here We Go 'Round the Mulberry Bush."
- Think of an additional verse for "Here We Go 'Round the Mulberry Bush" by adding another action, for example, "This is the way we tie our shoes/pet the dog/eat our lunch," etc.
- Read through "Two Little Dicky Birds," and then read it again, this time asking your child to act out the second verse.
- What kind of music would Old King Cole dance to? Would it be happy music or sad music?
- With your child, find three words that involve sound, for example "sing," "hush," "tap." Can your child make the appropriate sound each word suggests?

- Which one is your child's favorite nursery rhyme? Why?
- Can your child identify a noisy nursery rhyme? What about a sleepy nursery rhyme?
- Which nursery rhyme character would your child most like to be? Miss Muffet? Old King Cole? Wee Willie Winkie? Why would your child like to be this character? Can your child draw a picture of his or her chosen character?
- Read "Hush, Little Baby" to your child, stressing the last word in the first line of every verse. Ask your child to clap when he or she hears the corresponding rhyming word in the second line.
- Read "Girls and Boys Come Out to Play." Ask your child to point to the words that rhyme with "play" (i.e. "day") and "call" (i.e. "all," "wall"). Does your child know any other words that rhyme with these words (for example, "may" and "say," "ball," and "tall")?
- Can your child paint a picture of the dreamland tree in "Sleep, Baby, Sleep"?